Lovers, Ci

Molly Smyth was b......
Liverpool and lived in London for most of her working
life. She returned to Liverpool and died on Merseyside
in 2014.

Lovers, Ciggies and a Decastitch

Molly Smyth

Co Loa Media

First published 2015 by Co Loa Media

Co Loa Media
Cheltenham
GLOS
GL52 2DA

ISBN: 978 0 9928962 3 2

Designed and typeset by Co Loa Media
Printed in the UK by Anthony Rowe

For Ginny Smyth (née Murphy)

'Be humble
always be humble.'

Miguel de Unamuno
Christ of Velásquez (1920)

CONTENTS

Judith 32
Alma 33
Jade 34
Therese 35
Annette 36
Bernadette 37
Becca 38
Bella 39
Portuga 40
Cassie 41
Kassima 42
Ruby 43
Nava 44
Rona 45
Janey 46
Jessie 47
Anais 48
Lily 49
Brigitte 50
Julie 51
Amelie 52
Nicole 53
Millie 54
Olga 55
Tullia 56
Anna 57
Jenny 58
Mona 59
Paula 60
Kathleen 61
Pelona 62

Eugenia

No fire or blue mornings
raises the sheets
of my lover's bane
chasing numbers with the wind
smoking a cigarette
bowing out as she came in
the smell of rain
she says,
like some celebrity.
'I want to be free.'

Anneka

I could live like Sylvia Beech
while you did your designs
we could sip *Laperouse Syrah*
we could swank real fine
dip our *moule* in garlic
sit down with policemen
and discuss our latest role
fidget with polished fingers
dance on the Boulevard
tick off the meter.

Ginny

•

Tell me I was useless baby
amid the falling rain
oestrogen in the dilatory light
accents from Crossmaglen
doctors grin, sisters delight
tell me I was useless then
the might have beens
and 'ifs' of history
how love only grants us
three missed trains.

Nika

The brown river
is calling me home
crickets turn electric
birds thrum the dusk
my lover's dance
and drumming fires
the sourball colours
of an Indian summer
do only children laugh
in the long grass?

Valera

In the garden
my lover sleeps beside me
my son gone back to his father
days fire a troubled warming
salt rims the earth
not like her
who scatters easy
the fruits of women
the *poetes maudit*
she always loved.

Blue

I think of you when
blue is in the trees
when winter fires the dusk
a tattered sheepskin
hanging to your knees
your stolen boots from Hugo Boss
you say, 'I'm aching for a baby'
and roll your eyes to the Irish Sea
a dice flung laughter without the fury
at all I love the most.

Wenda

Tell me I was useless
across the Peloponnese
when we drank at evening
beside a shining sea
useless the translucent weed
you squeezed across your belly
dripping yellow, calcium, you said
for the baby
after *in vitro* fertilisation
there would be no need.

Yolanda

You say I sip wine and stare
and have people think
I'm interesting but
you say you're not convinced
I never liked holidays
I never took you on one
nor your son
you dance by the sea
she turns you on
don't make me swallow!

Yanna

My lover weeps, 'You don't even try'
her pen goes scratch, scratch, scratch
her garden shifts in the evening light
her dog lies awake near the fence
in her hair, in her eyes
a bitter dance
'we're history' she sighs
the pen continues the manifest
please stop writing lady
you're a fool to leave.

Loyola

She was never obscure
nor particularly driven
but pretty Jewish
in what she was doing
and knew in her heart
she was just a part
of something bigger
between home and distance
was a basic theorem
love the one who loves her.

Poeta

Hard men, carpenters
retired now, still big jaws
on the bus laughing,
down the hill, skilled,
terylene trousers
starched shirts, reposed
gnarled hands, time served
houses bought, Protestants
another life, mother's words
never to this door.

Phillipa

That artist photographer
the one who knew Antonio
who now lives in California
he filmed our street once
and captured his father,
a customs official, slope shouldered
stepping from the bus
who walked like a dead man
beneath evening trees
home to his wife and family.

Eileen

It's important to know
where you come from
I remember my mother
boiling the washing
in a copper
that was new then
compared to the bath
houses on Beatrice Street
my Nana used to use
which sheets do I sleep in?

Rosa

Your hips are gentle
I forget about mountains
and sunlit hills
they swell the hubbub
of a crowded bar
a wine to sip
watching you sing
a cigarette to smoke
after kissing your lips
a kindness to continue with.

Hannah

Mary the Catholic Queen
would not let them
spit saliva into the gob
of her baptised son James
common for left footers
and Scots at that time
I stood by an unlit lamp
waiting for my lover
a tree, a bridge, the rain
childless again.

Sandra

Geese fly a leaden sky
over my shoulder, barren
sloping, honking
to the New Year,
no fire or blue morning
comes between my lover
and the sea
she goes as she came
uncertain of my name
smoking a ciggy.

Inga

Who wouldn't worry
about what we've shipped
or what we're doing
with women we love
pulled from dull marriage
uncertain dread
the scary depths
can anyone remember
a singing brightness
that nearly floods us.

Magdalena

You were so at ease
right from the start
you turned me on
your Ma, crawls to Santiago
from the airport on her knees
grateful to be born
in the oranges and morrena
am I lucky or just troubled
is that why I fight so hard
to make the pudding.

Cara

Here we are again
sitting in the sun
watching the kids run
on the ferry
summer gone without her
then my son says
'she loved the horses'
he's finding his feet
and I start crying
going back to Ireland.

May

Winter 1918 - 2007
smoking a cigarette
going out as she came in
chasing numbers
with the wind
a smell of snow
the same calendar
as Ingmar Bergman
her daughter says
'she'd gamble anything.'

Antonio

All poets die intestate
what a rock'n roller you are
throwing rages at your kids
at my lovers
all your troubles
your disappointed eyes
your could have beens
if it wasn't for me/ can't you see
for a photographer
this isn't your picture.

Linska

I dance with my will
with my heart, my teeth
I rip out what others don't see
tears, depressions, drudgery
the image vitiates me
when you see a ballerina still
glamorous, perfectly poised
there is always another reality
1963 was a big year for me
I married Antonio Lorrazzi.

Faith

All the schools along that line
what are they learning
when the ships stop coming
then a story suddenly appears
Kobe, Manila, Barcelona
the times you've lived and died
teach your kids
don't mess them up
no singing sea ports
no laughing rivers.

Christine

Looking at the river
I've forgotten what I've read
remembered stuff forgotten
don't remind me what she said
strings of seaweed cling to me
bottles, starfish, tidal wood
this lonely beach, in my head
most of it rotten
died alive, still kicking
when you waved ta ra.

Cassandra

Sitting here in Puerto D'Angele
the San Carlo Metropolitani
Napoli before me in evening sunlight
Campari, Moschinos, Italian leather
Giuseppe Verdi, wicked glasses,
is it me who draws attention
sheathed to foot in Egyptian cotton
or catches the whisper
who do you think you are,
better than your Da or Ma?

Diane

Sipping wine from a cask
or reading a book
she's there, she's everywhere
inside me, in the sea,
the dancing tide
her eyes remind me
of the world inside but
infidelity that place, that time
who can live like that
my lover asks?

Mary

When the kids are looked after
when all the loving is done
when every part of perfection
has drained from a perfect sun
please leave me the sea
and your blessed mother
a horizon to pray upon
an altered state, a naked moon
oblate through a window
to dance again.

Phoebe

What's best in medicine
like a prayer
or meditation
is taking it one at a time
strapped to a rocking chair
on a trapeze
off my face
on smoke and wine
not looking down
measuring distance.

Juna

By the lovely gardens
of Saint Phillip Neri
Our Lady waits on Catherine Street
in one hand she carries
fresh linen and eau de cologne
in the other, the soul of my dead baby
she smiles, her ravaged face
luminous as the moon
and shares her love
on public telephones.

Farina

Fat men gulp *fino*
white faced dineros
dark glasses suck *gambas*
unwashed chancers
shout *mas vino, tapitas*
at unshaven waiters
men who have never
made beds, washed dishes
but know about horses
watch me dancing.

Jennifer

I feel your silent anger
it always makes me suffer
our life between the covers
what's wrong with loving
the dead
or venerating your Papa
what you don't do I guess
is tell him all your troubles
or what he does
beside you in bed.

Judith

The psychiatrist says
'try to distance yourself
from extreme emotion
it's not the Russian Federation'
my husband hangs his head
a fly in his web
he thinks
'you don't need to be
clever to tell her that'
I'm a fool he wagers.

Alma

Do your eyes twinkle at
the dance of Thebes
where we lay on the beach
at Seaforth
on wrinkled sands
you grabbed my hand
and guided me through trouble
my sanctity gone
you held my face
against the moon.

Jade

Can we construct a story
from moments of doubt
awash in telephony
we call upon lovers
their slumbers a polysemy
chained to the sea
my greatest days
without a care
make no sense to me
without a prayer.

Therese

A drop of blood
reveals your forehead
don't crash this door
she is not there
nor in the sky
nor on the earth
the owl, the wolf, the vole
the moon, a ship, the sea
but inside us all
says Teresa d'Avila.

Annette

An evening sea house
wood and painted white
a picket fence outside
like Anne Benson's poem
love and afternoon laughter
a late sun
shallow surf on the strand
yellow sand
books we read together
before it all fell in.

Bernadette

I'd give my eye teeth
to see that place again
holding hands by the bridge
where the river bends
clear as Brooklyn
in fine weather
the evening Paul Simon wrote
Homeward Bound
dreams we dreamed
literature our mirror.

Becca

You've been lonely
who hasn't
but you have a new
friend now
your lover sits
beside you
is she thinking
how to explore you
drink more drink
lucky dip you?

Bella

A sea rose taken
from the river Alt
a warm upstairs
kids and dogs
is that what you want
a house and a husband
who bellows *basta*
and serves the pasta
with love and tomatoes
does it scare you?

Portuga

You wave me off
and life is sad
you help me realise
what I do not know
no religion
south of the belly
a frozen Atlantic
a wind lashed howl
your fierce kisses
warm Cape Verde.

Cassie

Bilbao and Guggenheim
white across the Nervion
rain and bridges
the ships go under
sometimes in sun
always the Chubasco
you start to laugh
at a marshmallow bar
your maritime cathedral
dances on water.

Kassima

That poverty you spoke
of yellow and grey
under the sun
you're different here
on the Mersey
at Kerry's musical clubs
The Iona and Taxi
Linacre and Melrose
but you shiver like Camus
at the desert.

Ruby

Bathing lightly she emerges
fragrant, cold and furious
'some pillow talk you have'
she says, then
'don't you want to eat with us'
she phones the St Petersburg
and quieter her *Other*
donning furs and boots
we go to attend the dinner
my lover of ten winters.

Nava

You glide between two lovers
up by mother's church
sunlight swathes the flowers
how beautiful your dress
this side of the river
this side of the tracks
your lace covered arms
your eyes like fireflies
dance like satyrs
this Sunday in summer.

Rona

A hot spring day
in Liverpool
she gets on the bus
humming a tune
she could have been
from Vera Cruz
the way she looks
the way she moves
black and seventeen
and nobody's fool.

Janey

Who hasn't thought
beneath the stars
about who we are
and what we're doing
or what we're going to do
'one thousand nights'
you whisper,
'I spent with her
can you love me
the way she used to?'

Jessie

Half past eight
waiting at the bus station
a whole day to kill
untwirl a *Buckfast*
a wee kingdom
as they say in Glasgow
if you come back
you said you would
but I'm not betting
your horse will run.

Anais

The fine evening light
when the cloud breaks
and shines the incoming tide
like an arriving freighter
why did it take you so long
to call my name
or look this way
like a car filling up its lane,
by the *Adelphi*
the pavement is green.

Lily

Antonio used to say
the scent of a woman
is heaven for any man
absent
love has a feature
like luck or a number
when you have it
do you wonder
do you feel strong
do you need it?

Brigitte

What is the point
where is the goal
the nets, the white lines
the sun, the ball?
All there seems
is a wooden cross
and your face
painted upon it
a Pickford's van
going down the road.

Julie

When she comes home
one sea green evening
the wood yards shake
Seaforth rises to greet her
every bar makes her laugh
each tune plays her lips
Oh it's a trip, she loves it here
she wakes next day
to a dawn novena
and wonders.

Amelie

My great month January
my best day Monday
I rest supplicated
all fires extinguished
the coastline safe
from consumptive friends
the silent majority
who set their time
but not by me
my weekend sings.

Nicole

A shiver in getting to know you
walk the beach La Rochelle
lunchtime
peche frites, wine, siesta
see the kids laughing
bathe in turquoise water
Martini, Cinzano
Diner et promené,
deux expresso
do you want me as a lover?

Millie

You crossed yourself
and said *c'mon love*
let's tie the knot
were you so brave
in that same sun
when I was young
the kids just born
the house in ruin
my life in the *Mulliner*
all boarded up.

Olga

I lie by the river
under the sky
and wonder
by the tulips
was it the tide
that brought you
or the Gods
of brine and piss
a bottle in your bag
to fly between us.

Tullia

There's a ship, a map
a miracle of small design
I want to get out, leave
do my own stuff
that's the trouble
with men
they don't know enough
it makes me want to cry
or wonder
is it like this everywhere?

Anna

The inventive west
does not care
at how we spend
our time
blowing our brains out
bad wine, bad breath
we want to dance
when the wind blows dust
and death
across our land.

Jenny

A universal song
a grain of sand
you don't mind
leaning backwards
blossom trees in spring
the yellow light
Tesco's at midnight
your hand
hidden by shadow
my defences down.

Mona

Listening to the rain
we shuddered at the thought
of the next arrangement
another down payment
a girl with the long gait
and turned down lips
a hunted look
that makes you scared
remember her when young
then she smiles.

Paula

The moon cradles us
the smell of wood
magnolia, cotton and tar
perfumes the night
all washed down
we descend to town
the radio sings Aretha
lover take your time
New Orleans below us
is like a hammer.

Kathleen

She caught me dancing
by the Northern Line
she said she lived
on Hampstead Heath
but her clothes were
from another scene
more like Camberwell Green
then she screamed
'give me back my fucken
demons'.

Pelona

She sees
the evening light
cross yellow block
paying debts
to shadows of society
lilac as the night
between five and eight
she phones the kids
the bars a clock
the walls a life.

Christiana

Are you just a wipe
across my windscreen
a bleep
on my credit system
an extinguished flame
between us
will you show me
the beauty of Aquinas
the consoling love
of your freedom?

Pascal

You were so free
standing wide eyed
like a GI bride
to sing for us
that time in Paris
the year *Lady* died
it's quiet where I live
I'm shrunken now
but I still hear your song
whisper in trees.

Juana

It's September here
I'm lucky to survive
your Ma, all scorn
crawls to Mass
for holy communion
to shake me loose
just her desire
to keep hold of you
but I'm the jug
and you're the wine.

Beatrice

What was I doing
with a woman like you
Jesus, that time
you drew my confession
I didn't love anyone
a fish knife
bone handled, ice cold
pressed to my thighs
you dragged it from me
a needle truth.

Dina

We who have broken
dreams or given notice
of the burdensome toils
that bear us alone
generally gone midnight
to where light puddles
the drugstore window
becalmed, we make for
the Pharma counter
our dawn all smiles.

Rita

You were swaying
and then embracing
me across the floor
your face a mirror
your eyes fixed over
you grabbed my hand
and ran it through
your ribboned curls
you kept me dancing
until it hurt.

Tamsin

With your dry biscuits
and chocolate swirls
and your cookies
you eat by the bin
what's that about
why are you so hungry
you were never that girl
go and see someone
don't leave your dreams
with nursing assistants.

Billie

A morning tub of semen
an oestrogen test
embryologist's delight
'Here's another egg
heh, heh, hurray'
it's not worth a light
but she looks fine
she's happy, hey
what's not right
amen sunny day.

Carina

I heard coming home
a midnight train
and a young woman
from Pendino
who talks of a writer
called Elena Ferrante
and kisses me quietly
on St Anthony's quay
she laughs in the silence
it makes me die.

Carmen

I stood by an unlit lamp,
a tree, a bridge in the rain,
please baby give me a sign
waiting by the tracks
on a Sunday afternoon
then a story appears
your face a picture
a girl of the tenements
full of adventure
your running hair.

Mo

She finds an oasis
away from the river
in Valencia there's a Bodega
behind the cruise terminal
her aching body
crawls towards it
she pays her entrance
gives money to the vagrants
says a prayer for her daughter
lays her head on a table.

Angelica

You bring her near
to warm her fingers
around your fire
then you realise
by springtime trees
you don't know her
not at all
you know fuck all
but the flame's still yours
to give or burn.

Carrie

'We saw her today
wow she dances those stairs
what's her name Frankie
what flag has she unfurled?
She sways this way, that way
she never did that with you
you didn't treat her right
that woman loved you
she's happy, let her go
you were never right.'

Patsy

Smell of salt sunrise
the river, seagulls calling
for Catholic Labour
and a Democrat
he'll always stand another pint
but these days are not his own
his lovely daughter
fresh and alive
skips in the waves
holds me tight.

Julia

She sits astride the dunes
ships creak on their chains
it isn't me who whispers
'God is not afraid
there is a love inside'
she scours my eyes
laughs at my surprise
anchors bind my feet
is it me you see
rocking in her arms?

Maria

No matter what she sings
in the cold light of spring
indifferent stars
surround her
and let her know she's free
no matter what she sings
the unfolding earth
holds her heart
she loves this time
at Easter.

Greta

Tell me where's my baby
tell me what the doctor said
I carry your love inside me
finding in the cradle
a loss to the morning infirmary
the dawn and falling rain
you look away beside me
the song of Michael Fury
haunts the Irish sea
she is gone from us.

Phoenicia

We fix our yellow star
towards the inventive west
the sky looks down in wonder
at how we spend the time
on a ship, by a map
with a bottle that's the trouble
will we know
if there's more to come
a sail that makes us run
or separates our best.

Donna

Glasses shade your eyes
silver cups your ears
heavy, scarred, good looking
fighting against the tide
your battered, brigand years
you stride to close the gate
the tremble at your thighs
closer to the heat
your lover somewhere hides
from freshly laundered fears.

Sarny

Somewhere beyond her boasts
inflated or in despair
a life without prayer
missing out from property
the love of dogs
better than any woman
then there was her mam
a bitter cadence of the East Coast
who knew little of the Odyssey
that couldn't be bought.

Marsha

Does it make you sweat
rubbing stones beneath a sun
trying to get a blaze going
at just what we've done
is it necessary to dance alone
in the yellow light of spring
acting out a single love
or spend a life
maybe a lifetime
learning to live?

Harvest

Nothing defines us like hope
even tho' places we've sworn
never to return
there is always a river
running through our souls
here is the Alt before the tide
and on blackened wood
the cormorants we heard
cry last winter
who will tend our bones?

Frankie

Hightown smells of salt
reeds reach out from the mud
a low sun covers my tracks
a red flag flies on a sandhill
how beautiful is love
this side of the river Alt
upstream is the Borstal
'it's all *me eye*'
young women say
dressed in silks and linen.

Mina

Hail Mary full of grace
beneath her pink pyjamas
the whirr of the morphine driver
is like a mosquito in deepening light
the manner of her passing
a quiet celebration
when she moans
'you're all miserable sods'
we thank you God
for the blessings you bestow.

Bridie

She died on the Epiphany
twelve days after Christmas
making her declarations
without fuss for the year
I can see her now
on the 17th of March
blowing out her cheeks
like a schooner to kiss
a shamrock pinned on us six
brought from the orphanage.

Francoise

Sunlight on the flowers
Freshfield groans with lavender
buddleia and straw
tussle by the railway tracks
pink lupins give me sympathy
they sway like guards
their faces ignore my arms
those old mineral lines
disowned by methadone
remember generous acts.

La Rosa

She is such a generous spirit
she brings me *Bollinger*
on Christmas Day
we lie in bed laughing
she is like a gift from the sea
can we ever make history
in circumstances of our choosing
the light shines cold on her glass
Count John McCormack
sings *Ave Maria.*

Sadie

At just this instant she
tries inside to fix a place
where she won't feel it
and knowing her luck
a punter
in every room
hotel lounge
flophouse drum
she'll do what's necessary
that's the difference.

Milanka

What's wrong with dreaming
and loving the sea
you lift us up when life is sad
help us realise what we do not know
white hotels like sugared almonds
soften the sun and water
lovely young women laugh
with rich old men at the museum
men who want to love again
eat calf's liver.

Mardou

In the rain by Stirling station
waiting by the tracks
a woman, my lover
from Drumchapel
talks of Alexander Trocci
and his New York jacket
and Jock Stein's mate
whose daughter runs the Italian café
we were leaving for Glasgow
I was singing yeah yeah yeah.

Camille

We stood under a lean-to
waiting for my son
unlike Anthony Powell
and the one he'd 'put' to school
then sat, dreaming of Pliny
on a wall, listening to the rain.
I shuddered at the thought
of the next arraignment
at what else he'd done
my son, my freedom.

Biographical Note

Molly Smyth was born in Belfast in 1931 and brought to Liverpool aged two months from an orphanage in Ireland. Her mother Ginny Smyth (nee Murphy) had a sister, one of thirteen, who worked there and helped despatch unwanted children to Liverpool and American families. Molly was the last of six brought across the Irish Sea. Ginny Smyth used to prepare for her own 'trips' by steadily adding cushions to her waistline before the departure of 'the cattle boat' from the Princes dock.

Molly's father, John Smyth, a cooper from the 'Liberties' in Dublin had settled in Liverpool in 1905 and worked at the Bank Hall cooperage in the North End of the city. He was present in the 'second wave' of the general transport strike that gripped Liverpool in the boiling summer of 1911 and which led to the organisation of the casual trades all along the seven miles of the City's waterfront.

He died in 1935 leaving the family a rich cultural legacy but little in the way of money, swallowed by his lengthy bronchial condition. Poorly provided for, Molly's brothers went to sea and her sisters worked at factories in and around the docks.

Always being of an independent nature, a bit of a rebel, the youngest and spoiled especially when her brothers came home, Molly was a great dancer. She followed her sisters up and down the parishes and clubs of Bootle, Seaforth and Waterloo and then left Liverpool in 1950 to go and work in London. She had trained as a secretary, paid for by her brothers' allotment notes and by her mother's obduracy and was provided 'with something more than just tapping her feet'. Being the youngest, she was allowed to make her way. For the next forty years she lived and worked between Camden Town, Victoria and Hackney, 'a lifetime between the 24 and the 38 bus routes' she once said.

In 1963 she married the photographer Antonio Lorrazzi. It wasn't conventional. They had three children together over the next ten years. Lonely when she first arrived in London she embarked upon the extra mural programmes provided by Birkbeck College. She met friends there amongst women that were to last a lifetime. Throughout this time she continued with her dancing whilst holding down day jobs as secretarial support in offices.

At the age of 35 and with her first child a toddler (Peter Constantine) she took up an appointment as a low level clerk within the portals of the Home Office where she had been working casually since her son was born. She stayed there for twenty five years and rose steadily through the secretarial system to confirm the security her mother had craved, aided and abetted by increasingly progressive laws for working women within the civil service. But she never stopped dancing and going out. She loved her holidays in Spain.

Her husband turned increasingly to drink after the failure of his business and after a third child, a daughter Patricia, was born in 1973. The photography had started to diminish some years before this and the marriage became increasingly fraught with bitter episodes. This was not helped by Molly's increasingly open sexual intimacy with women from her college and dancing days.

Ten years later, she relinquished all rights to the house in Camden when she chose to live with her long time partner Sandra Gluckman in a communal house in Hackney. The children slowly followed her but made sure their father was looked after in his ailing years. They also were regular visitors to Liverpool when Molly returned alone some eight years later to care for her last sister who was dying of cancer. They remained in the metropolis to minister to their increasingly ill father, Molly stayed.

From an outline of this sparse history it would seem that Molly's richest life was spent on the outside, family, work, lovers, dancing. Apart from the Birkbeck short courses there is little trace of any formal education. Her large circle of friends would indicate a life lived in cafés, in kitchen parties, on dance floors in that quasi bohemian/suburban life many women are lucky enough or dread to live by - something that Molly was well aware.

Yet we have the poems. Throughout her life Molly never offered any of these for publication or sale. Her method of distribution was to post them to friends and relatives – often collected together on Home Office paper which made her laugh. There was never any danger of public recognition although she did once win a bronze medal from the International Library of poetry for the poem 'Blue'.

But the poems are important because of their almost prosaic frugality, the constant evocation of spoken rhythm and colloquialism – her frank and just treatment of sexual persuasion recognising both bohemian and suburban realities combined with her often esoteric but brilliantly alive sense of the modern; the sheer enjoyment of a cosmopolitan existence with a Liverpudlian sense of being.

Molly Smyth came from the working class and in many ways never left it but hers is not an epic of suffering and collective struggle but one of personal decision and unwavering hope. Her laughter rings along the lines of these pages in this her first book. Its lines reflect the laughter etched into her face and deep in those twinkling brown eyes. She loved a good argument as she did a drink and, of course, the eternal cigarette.

Molly died in January 2014 of the same cancer that afflicted all of her family. 'It just came for me later like a prostitute,' she chuckled and laughed in a haze of blue smoke. She did not really recover after a bout of 'flu in the autumn of the previous year but stayed quietly at home in the North End of the city that she loved so much. She spent her last weeks at a Catholic hospice not far from where the Mersey joins Liverpool Bay, looking out over the woods and big maritime skies. She took communion there each week until the day of her death.

Joan French 2014.